THE SPUD BOOK
101 Ways to Cook Potatoes

james houston t.
illustrations by chris jansson

SEVEN SEVEN
SEARCH
PUBLICATIONS
P.O. Box 252, Solana Beach, CA
92075

1st Printing, 1980

Seven Seven Search Publications
P.O. Box 252, Solana Beach, California 92075

©1980, James Houston T.

Typesetting by STATS Inc. of San Diego
Printed in the United States of America
Library of Congress Catalog Card Number 80-50166
ISBN 0-934726-01-9

HOLD IT!!!

— Don't turn that page. I didn't write all of this only to have you skip over it. But if you're *that* hungry and can't wait, turn to recipe number 54, fix a bite, and return here when you are done. ...Well, now you should feel better.

This book was written because I love to eat potatoes, and wanted to have a comprehensive collection in one place. Now I'm a great one for dropping a box full of recipe cards on the floor and then having to spend the next three hours sorting them back into place. By that time I'm so famished I'll eat anything — even one of the cards. Not wanting to establish this as a mealtime ritual, I decided to glue one end of all the cards together, and — *voilà* — a book.

As my collection of spud recipes grew, I was encouraged to shed my miserhood and share some of the recipes with friends and other potato freaks — like you. I have gathered old favorites from relatives, comrads, and strangers, and heaped them together with recipes I have collected and concocted through the years. The book you are now reading is the result of that effort and encouragement.

Now I'm not the gourmet type. I like recipes that are relatively simple — like me — and don't require an inordinate amount of time and effort to prepare. Who wants to slave all day in the kitchen, anyway — especially over potatoes?! I also want to serve food that is nutritious and not expensive. So, most of the recipes that follow are fairly simple and economical (my style), and offered with some emphasis on good food value. Besides, unlike gasoline, potatoes are neither expensive nor exiguous. That's why I've compiled a book on potatoes, not gasoline.

As with any cookbook, you have to remember one thing: all people's taste buds are not the same. Some may even accuse you of not having any at all, depending on what you serve them. So, if you happen not to like the way one or more of these recipes turn out — modify it to suit your taste; that's how new recipes are born. That's also how dynamite may be born, and why you need this book. But cooking is as much the "feel" and personality of the cook as it is a refabrication of facts and preparation statistics. So experiment and enjoy the creative experience of "food fixin'."

Dedication

Dedicated to the Lord
. . . Who created potatoes;

to Mom and Dad
. . . who taught me to like them;

to whoever invented jogging shoes
. . . so I can garnish my potatoes
` with all the calories I want;

and to Sherri, my wife
. . . who likes to eat potatoes with me
and faithfully stands by me

even through the garlic.

A special note of thanks goes to Chris Jansson, who scribbled the neat drawings interspersed throughout the book. Spuds everywhere are proud of you, Chris.

Many thanks also go to the numbers of people — listed and anonymous — who contributed recipes to this collection. Without them, you would have been stuck just with me and the way I fix potatoes. So lots of thanks go to these people for adding a wonderful variety and spice to life . . . and potatoes.

Contents

THE SPUD BOOK: 101
WAYS TO COOK POTATOES

Introduction

"What's for supper, hon'?"
"Meat 'n' potatoes," comes the All-American answer.

Regardless of the gender of who today's "hon' " is, one thing *has not* changed — potatoes make up a big part of the American diet. From vegetarians to hefty carnivores, virtually all of us consume potatoes — except, of course, those mistaken dietetics who are trying to eliminate the big calorie foods from their menus. Surprisingly, *potatoes are low in calories,* high in bulk — they fill you up — and, as you are about to see, a fantastic and versatile food.

Where do potatoes come from? Not to be outdone by those smartalecks in the crowd who crack, "from the ground," *Spud Book* facts show that more spuds are spaded in Idaho (where else?) than any other state in the Union, with a whopping 85,175,000 bags in 1976. Idaho is followed by Washington (55,800,000 bags), Oregon (28,913,000 bags), and Maine (27,440,000 bags). As a kid in Kansas, I also used to grow a few in my garden, so Kansas must be in there somewhere, too. In all, the United States produces about 354 million bags, or 16 million metric tons of spuds per year.

Continuing our school lesson a bit further, we now look into the exciting area of the *origin* of potatoes — which, unfortunately, is not clearly known. This, of course, means that God created potatoes, which the scientists are afraid to admit: ... "Scientific integrity" you know. For a complete discourse see Genesis 1:11-12, 29-30. Some post-Eden history *is* known, however, so read on.

Before the discovery of America in 1492 (when Columbus sailed the blue), the Spaniards invaded South America and found great quantities and varieties of potatoes under cultivation. They were called *pappas* by Indians of Chile. Because potatoes could be grown at much higher altitudes than maize, they were an important food staple in the Andean highlands from Colombia to Chile. The

marauding Spaniards are then thought to have carted the tasty tubers to far-off Spanish homelands before 1560. Many scholars, connoisseurs, and potato smugglers alike believe the potato to have then vacationed around Europe, inter-marrying with the locals and eventually making its way to Ireland, and from there to North America *(circa* 1719) as stowaways aboard a passenger ship. Accounts of Indians growing potatoes in pre-Colonial Virginia are generally regarded as inaccurate. Otherwise, how could we legitimately call the spud the *Irish potato* — unless the United States broke yet another treaty with the Indians? Yes folks, the potato *did* reach us North Americans because of Irish immigrants and is, thus, referred to as the "Irish potato" — notably so in the South in order to distinguish it from the "sweet potato." Wild in-laws of the potato are still found on elevated highlands of the Southwestern United States to the southern part of South America. Most of the wealthier ones, however, live in and around Acapulco.

Potatoes, like people, come in many beautiful sizes, shapes, and colors. The plants may be dwarf, short, medium, and tall. They come upright, spreading, or prostrate. The stems are round or angular, hairy or smooth, varying in color from green to different shades of purple to nearly black. Sound like some of your friends? The edible tubers differ in size, shape, depth of eye, skin, flesh color, texture, and composition. They can be round, oval, or long. The skin may be smooth, rough, or russet, with color varying from cream to brown, shades of red, purple and blue. The most common flesh colors are white and yellow.

Nutritionally speaking, the potato has approximately 90-100 calories, and a 75-80% water content. A spud has 2-3 grams of protein, 21-23 grams carbohydrates, and is essentially fat-free (unless you cook them in oil). Other nutrients include 9-11 milligrams (mg.) of calcium; little, if any, vitamins A, D, and E; .10-.12 mg. thiamine (vitamin B_1); .04-.05 mg. riboflavin (B_2); 1.5-1.7 mg. niacin (B_3); 20-22 mg. vitamin C, 115 mg. phosphorus, 1.2 mg. iron, 5 mg. sodium, and 875 mg. potassium, thus making potatoes a nutritious food. But a lesser-known quality of this vegetable makes them particularly valuable (other than being cheap to buy at the store, which *is* pretty hard to beat!).

Dietary fiber, or "bulk" and lower cholesterol levels

Studies have shown that many people can safely eat diets high in energy content, with a lot of that energy coming from the complex sugars, or starches (potatoes, cereal products). Physical activity (walking, running, work, even talking a lot, if you have a big mouth) plus basic body functioning can effectively consume the calories taken in, although is questioned by many *if it can indeed lower serum cholesterol levels in the bloodstream* — a low level of which many of those same people have. The solution? Dietary fiber, or "bulk." A logical and accepted conclusion is that protection against elevated cholesterol levels and obesity is afforded by a diet containing foods high in dietary fiber. A good source of fiber is the potato — *all* of it (ah-ah-ah, don't throw that skin away). Fiber is defined, basically, as the cell structure of plant substances that is not able to be broken down and digested by the human system. In passing through our digestive tract, it collects, absorbs, and cleanses out the residues and bacteria left in the tract. Of this fiber, there are three functional types:

(a) cellulose — acts as a moderate water absorbent in the bowel.

(b) hemicellulose — acts as a strong absorbent.

(c) lignin — not an appreciable absorber, but is thought to attach itself to and carry bile salts out of the body.

Potatoes have approximately equal proportions of all three!

Constipation and related complications (varicose veins, hemorrhoids), appendicitis, gallbladder disease, and diverticular disease are all accented — in some instances perhaps even caused — by a *lack* of regular dietary fiber intake. The best sources of fiber? Bran, fibrous fruits and vegetables and, yes, you guessed it, the potato! The moral of all this? *Eat them!* — they taste good and are good for you.

So we've just looked at some of the reasons *why* they are good for you (for a more comprehensive scope, ask a nutritionist, the Governor of Idaho, or a potato). So now let's turn to the best part — how to cook and make them taste good. That's what you're here for, anyway.

A Word About Butter

Just about all of the recipes that follow call for "butter." I like butter, and believe that it's better for you than margarines which contain hydrogenated vegetable oils — a process where the chemical structure of the oil is changed. Many authorities believe this process invalidates the benefits provided by vegetable and nut oils. Butter has undergone no such processing change. However, to provide the benefits that only nut and vegetable oils provide (linoleic acid, an essential fatty acid required by the body), we at our house melt one portion of butter and to it add an equal portion of peanut oil and safflower oil combination. Some people than add some liquid lecithin (the natural mobilizer of cholesterol), pour into a plastic tub, and keep cooled in the refrigerator (a necessity to keep your "butter" in a non-liquid state). An exciting and new taste sensation is created, it spreads easily on most anything, and it's good for you. It's all natural besides, so you won't upset the feelings of your potatoes. Thus, whenever a measure of "butter" is called for, use this mixture as you would any of the other stuff.

POTATO BAKE

Marylyn Murray
Leucadia, California

Not to be confused with *baked potato,* for those of you with a tendency toward spoonerism. I got this recipe from my good friend Marylyn, who seems to turn out something perfect everytime she cooks. Her husband — another Jim — couldn't agree more (and he certainly would if he could!).

What you need:
    8 medium potatoes
    3 or 4 green onions, chopped
    16 oz. carton of sour cream
    1 cup grated cheese
    1/4 cup melted butter
    1 can chicken soup
    1 cup corn flakes

What to do: Boil potatoes until fork tender, then grate coarsely when cool. Now mix in the chopped onions, sour cream, 1/2 of the cup of cheese, chicken soup, and butter. (Some garlic powder is good in there, I have found; but then, I like garlic in everything . . . almost!) Bake this for 1 hour at 350°. During the last 15 minutes, top the potato mixture with the other 1/2 cup cheese and the corn flakes. When done, serve it up!

2

POTATO VOLCANO

Vera T. (my mom)
Baldwin, Kansas

These taste great and I wonder why mom didn't fix 'em while I was growing up. Now she makes me fix them for her!

What you need: 4 or 5 medium potatoes
salt and pepper to taste
paprika
cream, or half-and-half
2 tbsp. butter
2 tbsp. grated cheese
ketchup or chili sauce

What to do: Boil potatoes until done, peel, and make mashed potatoes by mashing until fluffy, adding salt, pepper, paprika, and cream. Form into irregular mounds in a shallow baking dish. Make a deep indentation in the top and fill with a sauce made by creaming together the butter, grated cheese, salt and pepper to taste, (some garlic powder in there would sure be good!) and a dash or two of paprika. Then add enough ketchup or chili sauce to give a red color and heat (but do not boil). Fill the hole in the mound with sauce and place the dish in a very hot oven to brown. The sauce will bubble and flow down over the sides.

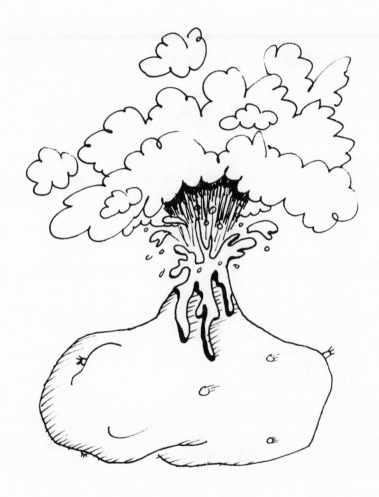

3 *POTATOES AND PARSLEY BUTTER*

June Coffelt
Denver, Colorado

Parsley is more than the only thing left on your plate when you go out for dinner. The flavor is unique, both raw and cooked into dishes, with its nutritional value superb. As you'll see here, parsley and butter makes a super sauce for spuds. Sensational!

What you need: potatoes — new potatoes are best
1/4 cup melted butter
2 tbsp. safflower oil
1-1/2 tsp. grated lemon rind
1 tbsp. chopped parsley
1 tbsp. chopped chives
1/8 tsp. nutmeg
3 tbsp. lemon juice
salt and pepper to taste

What to do: Boil potatoes until fork tender. While they cook, make your parsley butter by combining the rest of the ingredients. When hot, pour over the cooked potatoes and serve. Garnish with a hamburger.

POTATO CARROT MOLD

4

June Coffelt
Denver, Colorado

Not to be confused with the green substance that would form on potatoes and carrots if left out of the refrigerator for several weeks. This is a super supper dish, and combines two old favorites (which I always mash together anyway!).

What you need: 3 medium potatoes
3 medium carrots
1 cup warm milk
2 tbsp. melted butter
salt and pepper to taste

What to do: Boil potatoes and carrots together until done, and then mash. Combine milk, butter, salt and pepper, and heat until warm. Add to mashed potatoes and carrots and beat until fluffy. Using a greased baking dish, mold mixture into various creative shapes, such as small patties with spoon indentations in the top, or perhaps a scale replica of the U.S.S. Constitution. This dish is good served with a cheese sauce or tomato sauce. Bon appétit, or maybe bon voyage.

5

POTATOES QUICHE

Marie-Paule Achard
Concord, California

This one had to be translated from cryptic French by monks, to avoid letting it get into the wrong hands. I was still able to get it, however, so here it is.

What you need: 2 cups unbleached white flour
1/3 cup boiling salted water
2/3 cup melted butter
1 — 8 oz. carton heavy cream
2 eggs
1/2 cup grated Swiss cheese
1 cup grated raw potatoes with liquid squeezed out

1/2 cup or so chopped bacon or ham
salt and pepper to taste

What to do: Combine the water and melted butter. Cool some. Add flour, mixing into a soft dough with a fork. Once thoroughly blended, set in the refrigerator to cool and age for 30 minutes. With your new-found free time, mix the cream, eggs, Swiss cheese, and squeezed potatoes. Add salt and pepper to taste. Set this aside, too. Now take the aged dough and spread into a 9 inch buttered pie dish or a quiche dish. Place in a 350° oven for about 3 minutes. Take out, and, voilà! . . . warm dough. Prick holes with a fork in the dough. Place the ham or bacon in a layer in the bottom, spreading evenly. Now pour the other mixture over this and place back in your 350° oven for about 30 minutes, sprinkling with paprika, if desired.

KUKU SIBZAMINI 6

Fariba Basseri
Concord, California

This is an old Persian recipe brought to the United States on a diplomatic tour by Darius the Great.

What you need: 4 medium potatoes
6 eggs
1/2 tsp. each salt and pepper
1/2 cup olive oil, or favorite oil

What to do: Peel, boil, and mash potatoes. Place cast iron skillet with the oil over a medium-high heat, letting it get hot enough to "pop" when a drop of water is flicked into it. You, being quick and alert, will have already beaten the eggs, salt, and pepper very well. Add this to the mashed potatoes, and pour into the hot skillet like an omelet. Cover and reduce heat to medium. After 3 minutes or so, turn over (the eggs and potatoes, not you) — without tearing, of course! Let cook until golden brown. Slice like a pie and serve.

7

PORK 'N' POTATOES

Kaye Florance
Pacheco, California

Here's a favorite from my Uncle Kaye. Nothing she has cooked for me has ever been bad, not even that salty birthday cake. . . .

What you need: 4 medium spuds
1/2 pound salt pork, diced
1/4 cup chopped parsley
1 clove garlic, minced
2 pounds codfish, or similar fish
2 tbsp. olive oil
salt and pepper to taste
flour (optional)

What to do: Peel raw potatoes and slice. Mix pork, parsley, and garlic, placing half of the mixture in the bottom of a baking dish. Cover with a layer of half of the sliced potatoes, adding any salt and pepper you desire. Now break the fish into small chunks or flakes, and place in a layer on top of the potatoes. Cover with remaining pork mixture, adding on top of this the other half of the spuds, salt, and pepper. Add enough water to cover up over the last layer, then adding your olive oil. Cover and let boil over medium heat until potatoes are done. Thicken with flour if desired.

CHILLED GERMAN POTATO SALAD   **8**

Vera T.
Baldwin, Kansas

This is an old German recipe, and an easy one at that. Be sure to let it stand for a few hours in the refrigerator so the flavors will chill and blend. ("At ease" will be sufficient.)

What you need: 5 potatoes, boiled and diced
4 eggs, hard boiled and diced
3 sticks celery, chopped
1 onion, diced
1 bell pepper, diced
1 cucumber, diced
salt and pepper to taste
mayonnaise

What to do: When the potatoes and eggs have cooked and cooled, mix them (after chopping) with the other ingredients. Add your mayonnaise (3 heaping tablespoonfuls or whatever gooiness you desire), and blend in well. Chill.

9

CHOCOLATE POTATO CAKE

Kaye Florance
Pacheco, California

This is really good (like sour cream chocolate cake), so get ready for some good eatin'! You could even try making some mashed potato ice cream to go with it.

What you need:
    3/4 cup butter
    1-1/2 cups sugar — turbinado or raw white is good
    4 eggs, separated
    1 cup hot (boiled) riced potato
    1-1/2 cups sifted unbleached white flour
    2 tsp. baking powder
    1/2 tsp. salt
    1/2 cup cocoa or carob powder
    1 tsp. ground cinnamon
    1/2 tsp. ground nutmeg
    1/4 tsp. ground cloves
    1 cup milk
    1 tsp. vanilla extract
    1 cup chopped pecans
    cream cheese icing — my favorite

What to do: Cream butter and one cup of the sugar until light. Add egg yolks and beat well. Add potato and mix thoroughly. Add sifted dry ingredients alternately with milk, beating until smooth. Add vanilla and nuts. Beat egg whites until stiff but not dry. Gradually add remaining sugar, beating until very stiff. Fold into first mixture, and pour into a pan (13 x 9 x 2 inches), lined with wax paper (nifty anti-stick trick, huh?). Bake at 350° for about 45 minutes. Cool and gob on the cream cheese icing. Now invite me over.

10 *ITALIAN POTATO DUMPLINGS (GNOCCHI)*

Kaye Florance
Pacheco, California

Here's another one from Uncle Kaye. I think she is a part of a part Italian — or should be — and has come up with another yummy favorite here.

What you need: 4 large potatoes
2 eggs yolks
4 tbsp. butter, melted
3/4 tsp. ground nutmeg
salt and pepper to taste
1-1/2 cups unbleached white flour
1 tbsp. peanut oil

What to do: Scrub the spuds and boil until fork tender in lightly salted water. Peel while hot and mash thoroughly. Slowly add the beaten egg yolks, butter, nutmeg, salt, and pepper. Gradually beat in the flour. You should end up with a dough that is smooth and soft. Form into small balls and let set for a few hours. After they have rested, bring a kettle of lightly salted water to a boil, and add the peanut oil to it. Drop in the gnocchi dumplings and cook about 10 minutes. When done, they should float to the top. Drain and serve as a side dish to roast pork or beef, covered and lightly baked with olive oil, chives, and Parmesan cheese, or served with Italian style tomato sauce and Mozzerella cheese.

MOUSSAKA

11

This Greek favorite I first enjoyed at the now-famous Greek Festival in Dallas, Texas . . . I didn't know Greece was a part of Texas. . . .

What you need:
2 large eggplants
3 potatoes, peeled
2 large onions, chopped
1 pound lean ground beef
1/2 cup chopped parsley
1 cup tomato sauce
1/4 cup bread crumbs
1/3 cup unbleached white flour
2 cups milk
2 eggs
1/4 cup grated Romano or kefaloteri cheese
2 garlic cloves, minced or put through a garlic press (which gives a stronger taste)
1/2 tsp. ground cinnamon
dash nutmeg (to 1/4 tsp.)
olive oil
salt to taste

What to do: Slice eggplant, dry, and salt to taste. Fry in olive oil until browned; do the same with the potatoes, sliced 1/4 inch thick. Drain, and arrange 1/2 each of potatoes and eggplant in alternating layers in the bottom of a baking dish. Sauté onions in olive oil until soft. Set aside. In the remaining oil, cook the beef until browned. Add onions, garlic, tomato sauce, parsley, cinnamon, and nutmeg. Mix together well. Pour this over the potatoes and eggplant. On top of this arrange the other half of the potatoes and eggplant in layers. Beat the eggs and add the milk, flour, and bread crumbs. Pour this over the casserole and sprinkle with cheese. Bake in a moderate oven (350°) for 45 to 60 minutes. Cut into squares to serve.

12 *FRENCH FRIED BAKED POTATOES*

Vera T.
Baldwin, Kansas

Many people like to avoid lots of grease. To do that, you can do two important things: don't lubricate your own car anymore, and avoid eating fried foods — especially deep-fat fried foods. If you're like me, however, you love French fries, although with this recipe you eliminate 90% of the grease needed to cook them. Result? You get great-tasting french fries without all the grease. Hallelujah!

What you need: Potatoes, cut as for french fries
safflower oil, or other favorite oil
salt to taste

What to do: Oil the bottom of a baking sheet and roll the potato slices in it to lightly coat all sides. Pour off excess. Salt to taste and bake for 1 hour at 325°.

GARLIC SAUCE 13

Hazelle Carter

Serve this yummy sauce with fresh-sliced veggies — cucumber, cauliflower, carrots, etc.; fried vegetables — eggplant wedges, zucchini; and boiled shrimp and fish chunks. It makes an excellent sauce for fondue, and can also be used to get rid of that troublesome minty smell on your breath.

What you need:
1 large potato, boiled and mashed
12 slices white bread
4 cloves garlic
1 tsp. salt
1 egg
4 tbsp. vinegar
1/2 cup olive oil
hot water

What to do: Combine the garlic cloves and salt, and mash to a paste with a mortar and pestle (or substitute 1 tsp. garlic salt for the 4 cloves and salt, although the flavor will not be as fresh and strong). Beat in the egg and vinegar. Remove the crusts from the bread and crumble the slices into a mixing bowl; stir together with olive oil and 2 or 3 tbsp. hot water. Add bread to garlic mixture and continue beating. Add additional hot water until your concoction is the consistency of thin whipped potatoes. Speaking of potatoes, now add the spud you mashed earlier and beat until smooth. Makes about 2 cups. Dig in! Oops, maybe it should be "Dip" in!

14 *GRATIN OF POTATOES AND TURNIPS*

Hazelle Carter

For those of you who are crazy about cooked turnips, this is a great way to team them up with our favorite.

What you need:
    1 pound potatoes, peeled
    1 pound small white turnips
    6 tbsp. butter
    1 cup grated Gruyère or Parmesan cheese
    2/3 cup beef broth
    1/4 cup each heavy cream and sour cream, whipped together
       (1/2 cup total)
    2 small egg yolks
    salt and pepper to taste

What to do: Cut potatoes into thin slices. Boil for 5 minutes, drain, and dry on paper towels. Do the same with the turnips, keeping them separate from the potatoes. Use 1 tbsp. butter to coat the inside of a shallow baking dish. Arrange alternating layers of potatoes and turnips, dotting each layer with bits of butter. Season with salt, pepper, and cheese as you go, saving about 2 tbsp. of cheese for topping. Now bring the beef broth to a boil and pour over the potatoes and turnips. Bake at 425° for 45 minutes to 1-1/4 hours. Watch that the top does not get too brown. If it does, cover loosely with foil. Test with fork after 45 minutes to see if done. When spuds and turnips are thoroughly tender, remove from oven. Combine the cream and egg yolks, beat well, and pour evenly over the top of the vegetables. Salt and pepper to taste again, if desired, and sprinkle remaining cheese on top. Return to oven until topping is well browned.

CHICKEN AND VEGETABLE CASSEROLE 15

I can almost smell this one cookin' in the kitchen now. It's pretty easy to fix, and you can use left-over veggies, too. Serve with a big wedge of lettuce and hot sour dough bread. Ummmm.... What time did you say you ate supper?

What you need:
3 cups boned chicken
1 cup cooked sliced carrots
12 small white cooked onions
12 cooked potato balls
1 cup cooked peas
1 cup sliced mushrooms
4 cups cornflakes
4 tbsp. butter, melted
white sauce:
    6 tbsp. chicken fat, or butter
    6 tbsp. flour
    salt and pepper to taste
    2 cups chicken stock
    1-1/4 cups heavy cream
    1/4 tsp. garlic powder

What to do: Ahhh, you may be wondering what a potato ball is. If so, you make them by scooping out raw potato with a melon scoop and dropping them into boiling salted water for about 5 to 7 minutes. Voilà! A potato ball. If you're wondering what a chicken is, we're in trouble. If you are among those who command this knowledge, then arrange the 3 cups of boned chicken — no big chunks — in the bottom of a casserole dish. On top of the fowl, distribute in layers the carrots, onions,potato balls, peas, and mushrooms. Make your white sauce by combining the listed ingredients, adding the flour last and stirring it in gradually. Pour this over the other casserole ingredients. Now crush the cornflakes and toss in the melted butter. Sprinkle over the top of everything else, and shove into a hot oven (400° to 425°) for 15 to 20 minutes.

16 *SPANISH TORTILLA FOR ONE*

Claire E. Taylor
Concord, California

Claire learned this recipe as a young girl from her Spanish maid in Seville, Spain. Great for breakfast, lunch, and/or dinner!

What you need:　　1 large potato
　　　　　　　　　　2 eggs
　　　　　　　　　　1/4 onion, or green onions, chopped fine
　　　　　　　　　　salt and pepper to taste
　　　　　　　　　　Tabasco sauce

What to do:　Grate potato and set aside. Beat eggs in a bowl while you let oil heat to very hot in a skillet. Now mix together the eggs, potatoes, chopped onion, salt, pepper, and Tabasco sauce (a dash or two. Three or more if your palate is cast iron). Pour into the hot skillet and flatten into a nice pancake shape. Cook until golden on one side, then flip over and cook until golden brown on the other. Remove and add more hot sauce — especially if you need to stay up . . . or wake up!

NEW POTATO CASSEROLE 17

Now here's an easy one, and a great way to dress up those new potatoes.

What you need: 2 dozen small new potatoes
2 cans cream of chicken soup
1 cup grated American cheese
    (or 1/2 American and 1/2 Monterey Jack cheese)
1/4 cup diced onion
1 tbsp. butter

What to do: Boil spuds until fork tender and peel. Be careful not to burn your fingers! Sauté onion in butter until soft. Put whole potatoes in casserole dish and pour soup over them. Mix onion with cheese and spoon on top. Bake in hot oven (400°) for about 15 minutes. This dish is great without peeling the potatoes, which is the way I like them.

18 *NEW ENGLAND CLAM CHOWDER*

Hazelle Carter

What can be said about this old favorite except "superb?" . . . Enjoy!

What you need: 3 dozen large-shell clams
                (or three 8 oz. cans minced clams)
           1 — 8 oz. package sliced bacon, or 1/2 pound salt pork, diced
           2 medium onions, sliced
           2 tbsp. unbleached white flour
           5 large potatoes, peeled and diced
           1-1/2 tsp. salt
           1/4 tsp. pepper
           1/4 tsp. garlic powder
           4 cups milk
           1 cup heavy cream
           2 tbsp. butter
           paprika for garnish

What to do: Under running cold water, scrub the clam shells free of sand. In an 8 quart kettle over high heat, bring 1 cup water to a boil. Add the clams and heat to boiling. Reduce heat to low, cover kettle and cook just until clams are open — 5 to 10 minutes. Remove from heat. Pour off the liquid, but save it; cool the clams until easy to handle. Discard shells, or save to make earrings for your mother-in-law. Chop clams and set aside. In the same kettle over medium heat, cook the bacon until lightly browned; add onions and fry until tender — about 10 minutes. Gradually stir in the flour until mixed well. Now add enough water to the clam liquid to make 4 cups. Slowly stir this into the flour mixture. Cook, stirring constantly until slightly thickened. Now dump in the potatoes, salt, pepper, and garlic; cover and cook until potatoes are tender — 10 to 15 minutes. Add your chopped clams, milk, cream, and butter. Simmer until thoroughly heated — about 5 minutes — stirring often. Sprinkle with paprika, if desired, just before serving. Makes 14 cups or 8 bowls. You better invite that mother-in-law, too, after giving her those clam shell earrings.

POTATO CHIPS 19

If you think potato chips are good, wait 'till you have them home-made! These are great.

What you need: Potatoes — unpeeled
melted butter, or favorite oil
salt to taste

What to do: Slice spuds *very thin* with a potato peeler (unless you want potato chunks rather than chips). Place on a baking sheet or cookie sheet and brush with the melted butter. Salt to taste (garlic salt is really good). Place in a hot oven (500°) until browned.

20 *MANHATTAN CLAM CHOWDER*

Hazelle Carter

This non-creamy cousin of New England clam chowder is a great fireside warmer, or appetizer for any meal.

What you need:
    3 dozen large hard-shell chowder clams
        (or three 8 oz. cans minced clams)
    5 slices bacon, sliced
    2 cups raw diced potatoes
    2-1/2 cups diced onions
    1-1/2 cups diced carrots
    1 cup diced celery
    1 — 28 oz. can tomatoes
    2 tbsp. chopped parsley
    1 bay leaf
    1-1/2 tsp. salt
    1/4 tsp. garlic powder
    1 tsp. thyme leaves
    1/4-1/2 tsp. pepper

What to do: Under running cold water, scrub clam shells free of sand, grit, grime, and scum. In an 8 quart kettle over high heat, bring one cup water to a boil. Add clams and heat to boiling. Reduce heat to low, cover kettle, and cook just until clams are open — 5 to 10 minutes. Remove from heat. Pour off liquid, but save it. Cool clams until easy to handle. Discard the shells, chop the clams and set aside. In the same kettle over medium heat, brown the bacon, add the onions and fry until tender. Add the carrots, celery, and parsley; cook 5 minutes. Into your cauldron, now put the potatoes, clam liquid, tomatoes (and liquid), bay leaf, salt, garlic powder, thyme, pepper, and 5 quarts of water. Heat to boiling point, reduce heat to low, cover, and simmer for 20 minutes, stirring often. Throw in your clams and heat thoroughly — about 5 minutes — stirring frequently. Discard the bay leaf and dish out the chowder. Makes 14 cups or 8 bowls.

21 *BARBEQUED SPUDS*

This is an old Texas favorite I picked up while ridin' the range down there somewhere. Texas is famous for barbeque, and if you're gonna learn to eat it, you gotta know how to say it: baw-bee-k'you. O.K., you're ready to start.

What you need:
5 cups thinly-sliced raw potatoes
3/4 cup chopped onion
5 slices bacon, diced
1/2 cup grated longhorn or American cheese
1/2 cup grated Jack cheese
salt and pepper to taste
1 clove garlic, chopped or pressed
1 tbsp. unbleached white flour
1-1/2 cups scalded milk
1/3 cup ketchup
1 tsp. Worcestershire sauce
1 "shake" Tabasco sauce
2 tbsp. butter
1/2 tsp. paprika
chopped parsley for garnish topping

What to do: Fry bacon until crisp, drain, and set aside. Combine flour, salt, pepper, and paprika. Arrange potatoes, onion, garlic, flour mixture, and half of the cheeses in the bottom of a baking dish. Next, combine the ketchup, Worcestershire sauce, Tabasco sauce, and scalded milk. Pour over the potatoes and dot with butter. Cover and bake at 375° for 50 minutes. Uncover and stir. Continue baking uncovered until potatoes are tender — about 20 minutes. Sprinkle with remaining cheese, bacon, and parsley. Serve hot.

POTATO STUFFING FOR ROAST TURKEY 22

Very few people know of this excellent recipe for fantastic dressing. If that build-up doesn't at least get you to try it, tasting it certainly will.

What you need: 2 pounds boiled and dry potatoes — save the water in which you boiled them
1-1/4 or so chopped onions
1/2 cup butter, or peanut oil
5 cups bread cubs (half white, half wheat)
3/4 cup chopped parsley
1/4 tsp. garlic powder
salt and pepper to taste
3/4 tsp. poultry seasoning

What to do: Roughly mash the potatoes and add about 3/4 cup of the water in which you boiled them. Mix in well. Now sauté the onions in the butter (or oil) until lightly browned. Combine the onions with the bread cubes, parsley, garlic powder, salt, pepper, and poultry seasoning. Add this to the potatoes and mix well. Stuff turkey, or bake separately in a buttered dish at 325° for 45 to 50 minutes.

23 *BROCCOLI AND POTATO CHOWDER*

In case you're not big on clams, or they're out of season there in the desert where you live, brew up this tasty broccoli and potato chowder instead. Yummy in the tummy.

What you need: 2 pounds fresh broccoli, coarsely chopped
3 cups diced potatoes
3 cups chicken broth
1 cup chopped, cooked ham
3 cups milk
1 tsp. salt
1/2 tsp. garlic powder
1/4-1/2 tsp. pepper
1 cup half-and-half
2 cups grated Swiss cheese
1/4 cup butter

What to do: Combine potatoes and chicken broth in a kettle. Cover and cook until the spuds are nearly done — about 15 minutes. Add the broccoli, cover, and cook another 7 to 10 minutes, or until broccoli is crisp-tender. Now put in the rest of the ingredients and bring to boiling point. Reduce heat to low and simmer about 10 minutes. Sop up with some buttered sour dough bread. Man is that good.

BEEF STEW

This stuff sticks to your ribs.

What you need:
2 pounds lean beef, cubed
4 large potatoes, cubed
1-1/2 large onions, chopped in chunks
3 carrots, sliced thick
3 stalks celery, sliced thick
6 slices bacon, diced
1 clove garlic, chopped and pressed
1 cup fresh mushrooms, sliced
6 oz. tomato sauce
1 cup red wine
1/4-1/2 tsp. curry powder
1/4 tsp. thyme
salt and pepper to taste
1/2 cup water
flour

What to do: Fry the bacon in the bottom of a kettle. Coat the chunks of beef in flour and plop into the bacon grease with the bacon. Brown the meat, turning often. Now add the onion and garlic, cooking until onion is tender. Pour in the tomato sauce, wine, water, along with the curry powder and thyme. Cover and simmer for about an hour. Add remaining ingredients and cook uncovered until vegetables are tender. There you have it, pardner.

25 *GRATIN DAUPHINOIS*

Andreè Achard
Concord, California

This French delight serves eight, although when multiplied by thirty-six, could help feed the Dallas Cowboys. This is a good one.

What you need: 10 medium potatoes
5 large eggs
1/2 cup milk
butter
salt and pepper to taste

What to do: Peel potatoes and slice horizontally, about 1/8 inch thick. Arrange in two layers in the bottom of a shallow, buttered baking dish. Next, combine the eggs and milk and beat lightly with a fork. Salt and pepper to taste. Pour over potatoes, covering them barely. Dot generously with butter and then bake at 325° for 45 to 50 minutes.

PUNDT POTATOES 26

Mr. and Mrs. J. B. Pundt
Hemet, California

I met this sweet couple still on a honeymoon into their graying years. This old German recipe is simple, unusual, and unmatched in taste. It is only fitting that this specialty be named for these two vivacious, special people.

What you need: 4 potatoes
1/2 onion, chopped fine
6 slices bacon, diced
1 clove garlic, minced or pressed
salt and pepper to taste

What to do: Boil your potatoes, peel while hot, and mash well — adding nothing. In a skillet, fry the bacon, onion, and garlic, with salt and pepper to taste. Keep hot when done. On the dinner plate, place a big spoonful of the mashed potatoes, and with the rounded part of the spoon, make an indentation in the top of the mound. Now put a spoonful of the bacon mixture in the hollow and enjoy!

27 *POMMES DE TERRE PARMENTIER*

Andreè Achard
Concord, California

Don't worry if you can't pronounce the French name for this great potato-meat casserole. Just cook it and eat it. The only French you need to know is "ah-h-h-h!"

What you need: 10 medium potatoes
1 pound ground meat (beef or pork, or combination, or
lean hamburger)
1/2 cup cream
2 egg yolks
1/2 large onion, chopped
1 clove garlic, chopped fine, or garlic powder
salt and pepper to taste

What to do: Peel potatoes and boil 'till done. Shake dry and mash, adding cream and beaten egg yolks. Brown the meat in a skillet with the onion, garlic, salt, and pepper. When done, mix with mashed potatoes and scoop into a buttered baking dish. Bake at 350° for about 40 minutes, or until a light golden brown. Trés Bon!

SILVER DOLLAR SPUD PUFFS 28

Mr. and Mrs. J. B. Pundt
Hemet, California

Here's some mighty good eatin' whether you're passing through Reno or Muleshoe, and there's no gambling about the taste: great.

What you need: potatoes
                      grease
                      salt to taste
                      good appetite

What to do: Slice the raw potatoes like silver dollars. Leaving the peeling on is fine. Fry *slowly* in a skillet until done, but *do not brown.* Remove, drain, let them cool and become dry. The secret is to let them dry thoroughly. When cool, heat your grease to hot (about 450°) using a deep-fat frier if you have one. If not, use extra oil in your skillet so the potatoes can float. Drop the spud slices into the hot grease. They will cook fast and "puff out" quickly. Cook until golden. Remove, drain, and salt to taste. Be sure to let grease get hot again before putting in the next batch.

29   *POTATO NOODLES*

Boy are these good, and you don't even have to be *real* hungry to be able to dive into a plate full. It's one of those special kinds of tongue-smacking goodies, when served up with some creamed chicken or whatever.

What you need: 1 large potato
                      3/4 cup unbleached white flour
                      1 egg
                      extra flour
                      salt to taste

What to do: As you have quickly noted, this does not make a huge quantity of noodles. In case the whole crew has informed you they will be there for dinner, check to see that your spud supply is not running low, and increase the recipe. For the above proportions, however, boil the potato in lightly salted water until fork tender. Peel when hot and mash thoroughly. Let cool some as you beat the egg. Add this to the mashed potato along with any salt you like. Gradually dump in the flour, stirring as you go so the stuff doesn't get lumpy on you. You want to end up with a soft dough that is not sticky. Transfer the dough to a well-floured board, knead it some, and roll out to about 1/4 inch thick. Roll up like a jelly roll and slice every 1/4 or 1/2 inch. Now slice each little noodle wheel in half. Bring a pot of lightly salted water to a boil. Chunk all of the raw noodles into the swirling waters and cook about three minutes, or until they rise to the top. Drain and serve with creamed chicken (hint), or whatever else you like.

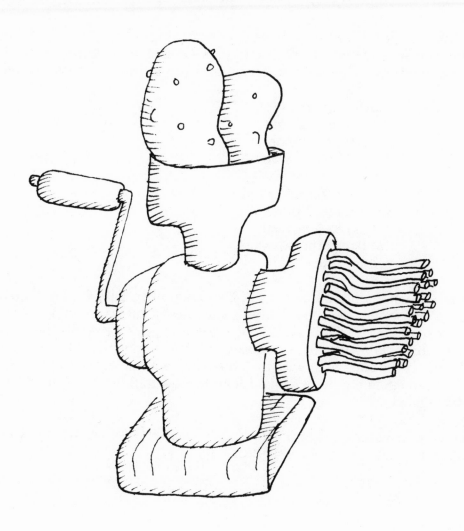

30 *DIET POTATO SALAD*

Since so many of our "diet foods" have everything fun taken out of them (with too much chemical junk added), it's nice to find one that is both yummy in the tummy and yet not crammed with calories. This one is fun to make *and* fun to eat!

What you need: 4 medium potatoes
1 medium cucumber
1 chicken bouillon cube
6 tbsp. boiling water
1 tbsp. mayonnaise
1 tbsp. chopped onion
1 tbsp. diced pimiento
1/4 tsp. celery seed
1/4 tsp. garlic powder
salt to taste

What to do: Cut potatoes into small cubes. Dice cucumber. Dissolve bouillon cube in a pan of boiling water, and then dump in your raw potatoes, cooking them 7 or 8 minutes, or until tender. Drain well, shake dry, and pour 4 tbsp. of the stock back over the potatoes, allowing them to absorb it. Add mayonnaise to the remaining liquid. Now mix the cucumber with the potato and add the dressing you just made, along with the remaining ingredients. Allow to sit 4 to 6 hours so the flavors will mix. Serve chilled.

(A good diet topping for a baked potato is some plain low-fat yogurt, a few drops of lemon juice, and some chopped chives or onion.)

VEGETABLE SOUP 31

Here's an American favorite which, if it's not *your* favorite, should be. There are many variations and concoctions called "vegetable soup," some of which actually contain vegetables. This one is a good one.

What you need: 4 potatoes, cubed
                    4 carrots, sliced
                    4 stalks of celery, diced, with tops
                    4 cups shredded cabbage
                    4 cups peas
                    1 soup bone for marrow and flavor
                    1/2 cup parsley, minced
                    1 onion, diced
                    salt and pepper to taste
                    1 clove garlic, minced fine
                    4 quarts water

What to do: In a kettle, sauté the onion and garlic in 2 tbsp. bacon grease or peanut oil, until tender. Add remaining ingredients except peas and parsley. Bring to a boil, then simmer until vegetables are tender. Do not overcook. Stir in the peas during the last 10 minutes of cooking, floating the parsley on top after serving.

32 *POTATO SALAD AND AVOCADO*

Anyone living in California learns to eat avocado on about everything. God made no mistake with this fruit: it goes well with many things, and you seldom have to worry about accidentally swallowing the pit.

What you need: 6 cups boiled, diced potatoes
2 tbsp. chopped onion
2 cups chopped green or black ripe olives
2 cups diced avocado

1/2 tsp. celery seed
1/2 tsp. dill powder
salt to taste
chopped parsley for garnish
1/2 cup or so mayonnaise
paprika

What to do: Mix all of the above together with your favorite mayonnaise, using the 1/2 cup suggestion as a guideline to suit your particular taste. Sprinkle with paprika and garnish with the parsley. Let set for 4 to 6 hours so flavors will mix.

POTATO PATTIES   33

Who hasn't had these? If the last time was when you were a kid and your mom fixed them for you, then you have really been missin' out in the meantime! So don't waste those extra mashed potatoes — whip up one of your old favorites, and maybe give someone else a fond memory of good family gathering around good food.

What you need: left-over mashed potatoes
                   optional additions: crumbled crisp bacon
                                        chopped onion
                                        grated cheese
                                        garlic powder
                   salt and pepper to taste
                   butter

What to do: Mold your left-over spuds into patties, adding any extras you like. Brown in the butter and be sure — at least once — to serve them up in the dark, early morning with eggs, toast, and the works. Who doesn't savor those kinds of memories?

34 *CORN AND POTATO CHOWDER*

Here's another chowder formula that is a winner when weather is cool and nippy, downright cold, or even warm to hot.

What you need: 1-1/2 quarts water
2 cups cubed potatoes
1/4 cup diced carrots
2 tbsp. (or more) chopped onion
1/4 tsp. celery seed
salt and pepper to taste
2-1/2 cups corn, fresh or frozen
1 tbsp. peanut oil or butter
1/2 tsp. savory

What to do: Into a kettle dump your water, potatoes, carrots, onion, celery seed, salt, and pepper. Simmer until tender. When done, add your corn, peanut oil or butter, and savory. Bring to a boiling point, then remove from heat. Garnish with parsley, dish it out, and gobble it up. Serve with some toasted garlic bread — ummmm!

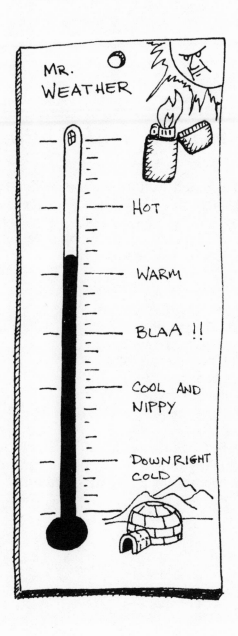

35 *HARD-TO-TELL SOUTHERN SPUD STUFF*

For this one, you just put in as much stuff as you like or don't like — but be sure to add some of each, at least 1/4 cup. It's hard to tell whether it will taste like the last batch or not, 'cause you have to experiment a bit to get your favorite combination. When you do, write the quantities down in the book here, and get ready for some good Southern eatin'. Really good up North.

What you need: _____ cup okra, washed and sliced
_____ cup canned whole tomatoes
_____ cup chopped onion
_____ cup corn, fresh or frozen
_____ cup potatoes, cubed
salt and pepper to taste
1/2-1 tsp. curry powder
1 clove garlic, minced

What to do: In a skillet, sauté the sliced okra, onion, and garlic, using bacon grease or peanut oil. When done, add everything else except the corn, cover, and cook until tender. Stir in the corn and simmer for a few more minutes.

ALMOST SOUP

Everyone has some extra spuds sitting around, and before they go bad on you, whip up this almost soup that is quick — sometimes — but always good. Don't forget to buy some extra carrots and have them sitting around, too, 'cause you'll need them here.

What you need: 4 medium spuds, diced
4 medium carrots, diced
1 large onion, chopped
1 tsp. garlic powder
salt to taste
4 tbsp. peanut oil
2 stalks celery, chopped
dash curry powder (more if you like it spicy)
2-3 cups water

What to do: Brown the onion in a saucepan using the peanut oil. When done, add everything else. Cover and cook over medium heat until vegetables are tender. Great to have on a rainy day.

37 BROWNED POTATOES AND ONION

Lots of onion makes any meal great as far as I'm concerned. This is a great meal.

What you need: 4 potatoes
4 onions
1 clove garlic, minced
6 tbsp. butter
salt to taste

What to do: Cut the potatoes and onions into chunks and boil in lightly salted water (many preferring to leave the onions in rings). Drain. Melt the butter with the garlic in a baking dish. Add the potatoes and onions, and coat well with the butter. Bake 1 hour at 350° or until brown and crisp, basting occasionally.

38 SAUSAGE 'N' SPUDS

Here is an economical way to have a meal in a bowl that sure fills you up. This is a Southern favorite I learned while growing up in Kansas.

What you need: 4 or 5 long brown polish sausages, or smoked, spicy sausage
6 potatoes, cubed
1 large onion, chopped
salt and pepper to taste

What to do: Slice the sausages into 1 inch hunks. Dump into a pot with the potatoes and onion, cover with water, and place on a medium heat. Boil down until potatoes are good and tender. Season to taste during last few minutes of cooking, and dish it out!

39

POTATO SPICE CAKE

Kaye Florance
Pacheco, California

Yes folks, you can even use those spuds to fabricate a fantastic flavorful feast finale to fit your fancy (make a dessert). Give this one a try — you'll be surprised. It's fantastic, fabulous, and fo on. . . .

What you need: 2 cups unbleached white flour
2 cups raw white or turbinado sugar
3/4 cup shortening
4 eggs, separated
2 cups mashed potatoes
1/4 cup cocoa or carob powder
2 cups nuts
1/2 tsp. ground cloves
1 tsp. cinnamon
1 tsp. nutmeg
2 tsp. soda
1 cup sour milk
2 cups raisins
1 tsp. vanilla extract

What to do: Cream the sugar, shortening, and egg yolks. Add the mashed potatoes and beat well. Add flour, spices, soda, and sour milk. Mix well. Now put in the vanilla, nuts, and raisins, folding in the well-beaten egg whites last. Bake 45 minutes in a greased, flat cake pan at 350°. Easy to make, huh? The eatin' will be much easier than that.

HOT GERMAN POTATO SALAD   **40**

Once you've had this, you'll know why the German people like their own cookin'.

What you need: 9-10 medium potatoes
6 slices bacon
1/4 cup chopped onion
2 tbsp. unbleached white flour
2 tbsp. raw white or turbinado sugar
salt to taste
1/2 tsp. celery seed
1/3 cup cider vinegar
3/4 cup hot water
dash pepper

What to do: Boil potatoes until done in lightly salted water. Drain and set aside. In a large skillet, cook the bacon until crisp. Remove the bacon itself when done, and into the grease put the chopped onion and fry until light brown. Stir in the flour, sugar, salt, celery seed, and pepper. Cook over low heat until bubbly, stirring frequently. Now add the hot water and cider vinegar, simmering until bubbly again — about 1 or 2 minutes. Remove from the heat. Crumble the bacon and slice the potatoes thin. Carefully add the bacon and sliced spuds to the hot mixture, stirring well. Heat thoroughly and serve. Ausgezeichnet!

41 *GETTING FANCY POTATOES*

These are fancy (and tangy!) enough to serve to royalty or in-laws, and taste good besides. The sauce does have a bit of a zing to it, so experiment with it first to suit your taste.

What you need: 1/4 cup mayonnaise (or with half sour cream)
2 tbsp. white wine
2 tbsp. Dijon mustard
6 large fresh mushrooms
1/4 cup grated favorite cheese
6 medium potatoes, boiled
2 slices bacon, fried crisp and crumbled
2 tbsp. chopped onion
2 hard-boiled eggs, chopped
1 clove garlic, minced
1-2 fresh tomatoes
paprika

What to do: Mix mayonnaise, white wine, and mustard in small pan over low heat. Simmer for 5 minutes and then keep warm. Make mashed potatoes with the 6 spuds adding, when mashed, the cheese, bacon bits, chopped onion, garlic, and egg (some people prefer to have already cooked the onion until soft before adding to potatoes). Separate carefully the mushroom stems from the caps. Set caps aside intact, and chop the stems, stirring in with the potatoes. Now slice the tomatoes into 1/4 inch slices. On your plate, place a tomato slice, topped with a mushroom cap (hollow side up), followed by a large spoonful of potatoes. Cover with a spoonful of the sauce and a garnish of paprika. Return to oven if necessary to get hot for serving.

42 NEW POTATOES AND LEMON BUTTER

Lemons are definitely more than the yellow wedge perched on the lip of your iced tea glass, or the description of your last car. They team up great with butter here to create another potato favorite you'll love. You do like lemons, don't you. . .?

What you need: 1 dozen new potatoes
4-5 tbsp. butter
1 tsp. grated lemon peel
2 tbsp. lemon juice
4 tsp. finely chopped chives
salt and pepper to taste
pinch nutmeg (don't let her slap you, though)

What to do: Boil potatoes until done. Drain and keep warm, yet do not peel. In a pan, heat the remaining ingredients, but do not boil. Cut the potatoes into fourths and add to the hot butter mixture, stirring to coat well. Serve hot. Goes great with fish.

43 BAKED DILL POTATOES

If you are a dill fan, and tired of dill pickles all the time, these are for you. This dish is fun to eat with fast music.

What you need: 4 cups diced potatoes
1 cup heavy cream
1 cup milk
1 tbsp. dill leaves
salt and pepper to taste

What to do: Place potatoes in a shallow baking dish. Season with salt, pepper, and dill. Next, combine the cream and milk, and pour over the spuds. Bake in a moderate oven (350°) for 30 minutes.

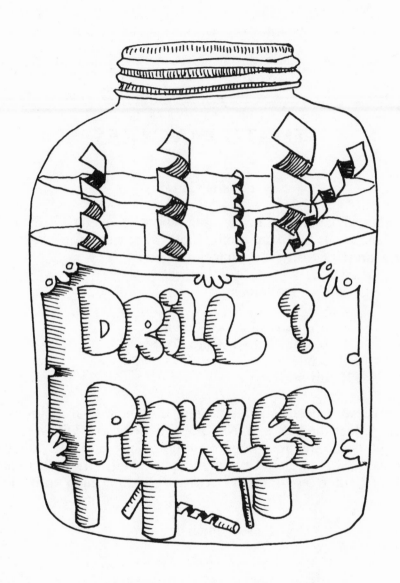

ARE YOU BORED WITH THESE?

44 *POTATO PANCAKES*

Hazelle Carter

Everybody has heard of potato pancakes, but few have taken the time to add a bit of adventure to their meals by fixing them. Spud cakes can be used as a side dish to about anything, and are really spud-smacking good!

What you need: 6 medium potatoes
1 egg
1/3 cup finely chopped onion
3 tbsp. unbleached white flour
salt to taste
1/4 cup butter

What to do: Wash and peel potatoes (saving the peelings for number 101), and shread (a blender does the best job). Next, beat the egg well with a mixer or elbow grease. Mix together the shreaded potatoes, onion, flour, and salt. Melt the butter in a large skillet over low heat. Pour several thin pancakes in the skillet and cook over medium heat for 2-1/2 to 3 minutes. Turn once, griddling each until golden brown.

HOT FRENCH QUARTER POTATOES 45

Hazelle Carter

These are great with gumbo and stuffed cucumbers. This is an old New Orleans recipe, where a fitting way to fix potatoes must be able to match the greatest gumbo in the world. Correct eating strategy is to dip the potato spears into the gumbo before each bite.

What you need: 6 medium potatoes
1/4 pound butter, melted
1 clove garlic, crushed
1/2 tsp. Tabasco sauce
cayenne pepper
paprika

What to do: Preheat oven to 400°. Wash potatoes but do not peal. Cut lengthwise into eighths. Score each spear into bite-size sections, cutting half-way through. Combine 6 tbsp. melted butter, the garlic, and Tabasco sauce. Brush onto the potato spears, then sprinkling each spear with a dash or more of cayenne pepper and some paprika, depending on how hot you like it. Bake in an open pan in the oven for 30 minutes, basting with the remaining butter half-way through baking.

46 *UNCLE KAYE'S HASHED BROWNS*

Kaye Florance
Pacheco, California

Feuds and wars have been started over Uncle Kaye's "hashies." All feuding promptly stops, however, when the platter full of potatoes is set in front of the clan. Try 'em and you'll see why. Making "hashies" is an art, however, and you have to know just when to turn them, and how high to have the heat while cooking them. No practice is needed to eat them; that comes natural.

What you need: potatoes — as many as your crew can eat
salt and pepper to taste
grease

What to do: Shread as many peeled raw spuds as you need. *After shredding, squeeze out the potato liquid.* Your hashed browns will turn out gummy if you don't. Over a medium to medium high heat, pour enough grease in a skillet to cover the bottom well. Pack the potatoes into the skillet after the grease is hot. Salt and pepper to taste. Let the first side get real brown before turning. After turning, brown the other side, making sure the potatoes in the middle of the clump also get cooked. This is why you pack the potatoes in the skillet tightly, not putting too many in the skillet so that the bottom browns before the center cooks. It's not as tough as it sounds, so don't worry. Serve piping hot, which is sure to keep peace in your family, too.

47 *MORE HASHED BROWNS*

There has to be a recipe for hashed browns using boiled potatoes, so here it is. These are great grubbin', too.

What you need: 4 or 5 medium potatoes, boiled and cool
                      3 tbsp. finely chopped onion
                      1/2 tsp. garlic powder
                      salt and pepper to taste
                      2 tbsp. butter
                      2 tbsp. bacon grease

What to do: Shread potatoes as you would cheese. Mix in the onion, salt, pepper, and garlic powder. Melt the butter in a large skillet and pack in the potatoes. Cook 10 to 15 minutes over a low to medium heat or until golden brown. Slice into fourths and turn each piece. Add the bacon grease now so the other side will brown, and cook until it is.

CREAMY POTATO PUFF 48

Karen Vensand
Encinitas, California

You can sure chow down on lots of this spud specialty, especially if you've got some barbequed chicken to go with it. Or you can easily forget the chicken and feast on the potatoes! Go ahead, no one is watching.

What you need: 4 cups hot mashed potatoes
1 — 8 oz. pkg. cream cheese
1 egg, beaten
1/3 cup finely chopped onion
1/4 cup chopped pimiento
salt and pepper to taste

What to do: Combine the softened cream cheese and potatoes, mixing well. Add the remaining ingredients and scoop into a casserole dish. Bake for 45 minutes at 350°.

49 *POP'S COUNTRY FRIES*

I remember the fried potatoes my grandfather "Pop" used to fix me when I was a kid. I would get to go stay all night with him, and wake up in the morning to the smell of these cookin' in the kitchen. It is with many fond memories of that wonderful old man that I provide this recipe to you.

What you need: 4 medium potatoes
1/4 onion, chopped
peanut oil (Pop used bacon grease)
salt and pepper to taste

What to do: Cover the bottom of a good old cast iron skillet with the oil. Over medium heat, throw in the onion and sauté briefly while you quarter the potatoes lengthwise, then slicing them sorta thin into the skillet. When all the quarters are sliced into the skillet, add about 3 tbsp. water and cover tightly. Let cook 5 minutes or so, then start turning the potatoes to keep from burning. The water steams the spuds and makes them crispy. Cook thoroughly and let them get good and brown. That's the way I like 'em.

50 *COTTAGE FRIES*

Cottage fries did *not* originate in the town of Cot, any more than Hamburger was created in the town of Hamburg. Be careful of what biased history books would teach you.

What you need: 6 medium potatoes (peeled, boiled, cool)
4 tbsp. butter, or 1/4 cup peanut oil
salt and pepper to taste

What to do: Slice the potatoes into the hot grease. Season with salt and pepper, cooking until golden brown. Many prefer to cube the potatoes rather than slicing flat. You take command of this. Add onion or garlic if you prefer. Cook over medium heat, stirring to brown all sides.

51 *OLD TIME MASHED POTATOES*

Here's a few pointers on a familiar old favorite way to fix potatoes. Pay attention, too.

What you need: 6 medium potatoes
1/3 or so cups milk
1 clove garlic
1/4 cup butter
salt and pepper to taste

What to do: Peel potatoes and boil in lightly salted water with the garlic clove. When done, remove clove, discard, and drain potatoes. A secret: *take the time to shake the spuds over heat to dry them out.* This makes them mealy and fluffy, allowing you to make perfect mashed potatoes instead of not-so-perfect gummy potatoes. Mash the *warm* potatoes thoroughly until all the lumps are gone. Now add your milk and butter that have been warmed (not boiled) together. Whip until fluffy, season as you like, and don't be a hog and eat them all yourself.

FRIED SWEET AND SOUR POTATOES **52**

Hazelle Carter

The sweet and sour tradition of the Orient complements very well the New World's favorite vegetable. Sometimes called "ah-so spuds."

What you need:　2-1/2 to 3 cups diced raw potatoes
4 slices bacon
1/4 cup finely chopped onion
1 tbsp. sugar or honey
3/4 tsp. salt
1/2 cup water (a little less if you use honey)
1/4 cup vinegar

What to do: Fry the bacon in a skillet until crisp. Remove and crumble well. Using 2 tbsp. of bacon grease, cook the potatoes over medium heat without turning, for 15 to 20 minutes, or until brown on bottom. Turn with spatula (unless you have real quick fingers), add onion, and cook another 5 minutes. Stir in the sugar (or honey), salt, and water. Simmer until potatoes are tender — about 15 minutes. Remove from heat and add vinegar. Cover and let stand for 15 minutes. Now remove the lid, add the bacon and reheat to serve hot.

53 *MASHED FARM POTATOES*

If you've ever worked on a farm, you know how hungry you get after a few hours work! These spuds will satisfy any appetite — providing you have enough of them.

What you need: mashed potatoes for 4
2 eggs
1/2 cup longhorn or Jack cheese (or combo)
butter
paprika

What to do: Heat oven to 425° to 450°. Beat the two eggs and shread the cheese. Mix into the mashed potatoes while they are warm. Put spoonfuls of the spuds onto a greased cookie sheet, making the "spoonfuls" as big or small as you like to eat. Brush the top of each with butter and sprinkle with paprika. Bake until light brown.

GOOEY POTATOES 54

This one is an old favorite around my house. It's simple — those are the kind I can understand — and fit most anyone's fancy, especially mine.

What you need: 6 spuds
                        1 pound cheese, diced (I use jack and cheddar)
                        1 onion, chopped
                        1/4 cup butter
                        1 tsp. garlic powder (or salt, if you like some salt)
                        1-2 tsp. bacon bits

What to do: Boil or steam the unpeeled spuds until done (slicing in chunks allows them to cook faster). Sauté the onion briefly in some of the butter, then adding the remaining butter to melt. Now combine everything but the bacon bits, and stir to let the cheese melt over low heat. When melted, add the bacon bits, stirring in well. Garnish with some paprika, if you like.

55

POTATO LOAF

When you grow up with lots of potatoes (they make great pets or neighbors, and they don't bite), they end up in most anything. Here is another terrific combination of delectables sure to please your palate.

What you need: 3 cups mashed potatoes
                      3/4 cup chopped, salted peanuts
                      3/4 cup chopped celery
                      1 well beaten egg

3 tbsp. butter, melted
2 tsp. grated onion
1/4 tsp. sage
pinch of paprika

What to do: Cook celery until tender in a small amount of boiling water that has been lightly salted. Drain and add the rest of the ingredients, mixing well. Pack into a greased loaf pan and bake for 35 minutes at 350°.

POTATO DUMPLINGS 56

Janet Barret
Cleveland, Ohio

This is an old Czech recipe from Cleveland, where bunches of Czechs checked in many years ago. This simple yum yum recipe is great with roast pork and sauerkraut. In making this recipe, some folks use raw potatoes, and some use boiled. You choose.

What you need: grated potatoes, 3 or so
flour
salt to taste

What to do: Mix flour and salt with the great grated potatoes until the consistency of soft dough. Take the lump of dough, roll in flour to coat, and with a large wooden spoon, lower into boiling salted water. Cook about 15 minutes, being careful to let the center of the lump get cooked.

57 *MEXICAN POTATO BALLS*

Hazelle Carter

The more Mexican taste buds you have, the spicier you may want to make these. Soberbio!

What you need: 3 to 4 medium potatoes, baked and hot
1/2 cup hot water
2 tbsp. butter
1/2 cup unbleached white flour
2 eggs
1/2 tsp. cayenne pepper
1/2 tsp. garlic powder
salt and pepper to taste

What to do: Scoop out the white centers from the baked potatos while they are hot. Mash smooth. In a pan, melt the butter with the hot water over medium heat. Add the flour, stirring well until all the lumps are gone. Add the eggs one at a time, beating constantly. Now combine this with the mashed potatoes along with the seasonings, mixing thoroughly. Shape into little balls, roll in flour or bread crumbs, and deep fry in hot grease.

58 CHANTILLY POTATOES

Vera T.
Baldwin, Kansas

There are some dishes you love now and wonder why you didn't like them as a kid. Remember? This is one of those for me. They are great and gooey — two ways I like potatoes.

What you need: 6 medium potatoes, peeled
1/2 cup milk
1 tbsp. butter
1/2 cup heavy cream
1/2 cup grated cheese
salt to taste
paprika
chopped parsley

What to do: Boil potatoes and mash with milk and butter. Salt to taste. Pile in a baking dish. Beat cream stiff, adding cheese and paprika. Spread over potatoes and place in oven at 350° until lightly brown — about 25 minutes. Garnish with parsley and serve.

59 SPINACH 'N' SPUDS

Sherri T.

When Sherri gave me this recipe, she was a Stokey. Now she is married to me, and it's a good thing — a real good thing — that she likes potatoes, too! I'm glad this recipe didn't change like her name did, 'cause they're sure good eatin'!

What you need: 6 medium potatoes
1/2 cup unbleached white flour
1 tsp. (or less) salt
2 eggs, slightly beaten
1/2 cup fresh raw spinach

What to do: Peel and cook the potatoes in boiling water that has been lightly salted, for about 20 minutes, or until fork tender. Let cool, and put through a sieve or ricer. Allow to stand a few hours uncovered until thoroughly dry. Add remaining ingredients, mix together well, and shape into small balls. Bring a kettle of water to a gentle boil, drop in the potato-spinach balls, and cook for about 15 minutes.

ITALIAN BAKED POTATOES 60

Hazelle Carter

Make yourself a great light meal by having one of these along with a big salad. . . . Italian dressing on the salad, of course.

What you need: baking potatoes
Italian dressing, or 3 cloves garlic crushed in 1 cup of peanut or
olive oil
foil

What to do: Using either your Italian dressing or the home brew made with the garlic and oil, put 1 tbsp. of the dressing into a square of foil. Poke holes with a fork into the skin of the baking spud, and then wrap it up in the foil, letting it rest on top of the dressing already in the foil. As the potato bakes, the flavors from the dressing are absorbed into the potato, and wowie!

61 *HERB POTATOES*

Vera T.
Baldwin, Kansas

These are good old Herb's last recorded words before he disappeared that wintry night back in '07, which is why we call these spuds by his fair name:

What you need: small new potatoes (red skins)
salt to taste
pungent herbs

What to do: Boil the new potatoes in their nifty red skins by placing them in a covered shallow skillet one potato deep, and using as little water as possible. Do not place potatoes on top of each other. Shake rosemary or other pungent herb over them generously. This will require a lot to penetrate the skins. When done, peel them if you wish, and brown or sear them with cream or butter. Spuds cooked like this and covered with lots of fresh dill are great with a fish dinner.

62

UNDIETETIC POTATOES

Sherri T.

Now not all people want the low calorie benefits of the spud, so they mx in various other goodies to increase the energy value available. Contrary to popular opinion, however — persons partaking hereof *DO NOT* commit a sin of greater magnitude than us plain potato people, so gobble away. . . . You still belong in church, though.

What you need: 1 pound potatoes
                     2 tbsp. butter
                     1 cup cream
                     1/2 cup consommé
                     1 tsp. tarragon
                     1/4 cup chopped parsley

What to do: Scrub, peel, and boil potatoes until done. Mash and add everything else listed above. Mix in well and serve hot. Great with roast pork or chicken. You might as well have some apple pie for dessert, too.

63

POTATOES IN CREAM

Vera T.
Baldwin, Kansas

You can make these in a big gob, or in individual servings. Taste best with any meal.

What you need: 4 medium potatoes, boiled and cold
2/3 cup cream
1/2 tsp. ground nutmeg
salt and pepper to taste

What to do: Chop potatoes and add the seasonings. Put into a baking dish or muffin tins. Pour an equal amount of cream over potatoes in each dish. Bake at 350° until light brown on top — about 15 minutes.

POTATO CROQUETTES 64

Vera T.
Baldwin, Kansas

These are sure a lot better than the potato puffs you find frozen in the store and they're also easy to fix, which means you're talking my language.

What you need: 2 cups hot riced potatoes
2 tbsp. butter
salt and pepper to taste
1/4 tsp. celery salt
few drops onion juice
1 tsp. chopped parsley
1 egg yolk
bread crumbs

What to do: Mix all the ingredients except the bread crumbs and egg, in the order given, combining thoroughly. Shape into small balls, dip in crumbs, egg, and crumbs again. Then deep fat fry for 3 minutes in grease heated to around 375°. When done, drain and serve.

65

POTATO DONUTS

Susan Caldwell
San Marcos, California

It took me a while to get this one, but it was worth it. This recipe has been in Susie's family for many years.

What you need: 2 cups lukewarm milk
1 cup sugar (raw white or turbinado is good)
3 eggs, beaten
1-1/2 pkg. yeast (dissolve in 1/2 cup warm water)
1/2 cup shortening
1 cup mashed potatoes
1 tbsp. salt
unbleached white flour

What to do: Into a mixing bowl dump your milk, sugar, eggs, potatoes, salt, and shortening. Mix, adding enough flour to make a thin batter. Next, stir in the dissolved yeast. Gradually add more flour until you have a nice dough — not sticky and not dry. Let rise until it doubles in size. Punch down (don't get too mean), and let rise a second time. Now roll out to 1/2 inch thick, cut into donut shapes, let rise again, and fry. When done, remove from grease and dip in sugar.

66 *POTATO SALAD*

My mom started feeding me this when I was a kid. I didn't quite go from bottle to potato salad, but almost. Spud salad almost always tastes best garnished with baked beans and fried chicken.

What you need: 6-8 spuds, boiled and diced
6-8 eggs, hard-boiled, peeled, and chopped
1 cup or so mayonnaise
1 tbsp. prepared mustard
1 small jar pimiento, diced
1/2 tsp. celery seed
1-2 tbsp. chopped sweet or dill pickle
1-2 tbsp. chopped onion
salt and pepper to taste
1/4 tsp. lemon juice

What to do: When making this recipe, use 1 hard-boiled egg per each boiled potato. Mix together the mayonnaise, mustard, and lemon juice. Combine with everything else, stirring together well. Let set in the refrigerator for several hours — even overnight — so flavors will blend. Remember the axion of the potato pledge: serve no potato salad before its time.

POTATO PYRAMIDS WITH ONION PUREE 67

Vera T.
Baldwin, Kansas

Yes, you guessed it — if it's with mashed potatoes, my mom is in on it. Coming from a part onion freak, this dish of hers is worth the extra effort to fix the onion puree, a task food processors have made much simpler. If you don't have a food processor, at least try to get some onion-proof goggles.

What you need: 2 cups mashed potatoes
melted butter
4 tbsp. grated cheese
1/2 cup chopped onion
2 tbsp. butter
1 cup water
1 tsp. cornstarch (if desired)
1 tsp. Worcestershire sauce
salt and pepper to taste

What to do: Make the onion puree by frying the onion in the 2 tbsp. of butter, adding the water and simmering until soft enough to put through a strainer. Add cornstarch (if desired) mixed with a little water. Follow this with the Worcestershire sauce, salt, and pepper, mixing well. Now shape your mashed potatoes into pyramids, brushing with melted butter and sprinkling with grated cheese. Put in a shallow baking dish and pour the onion puree around them. Bake at 350° until brown — about 20 minutes.

68

POTATO PUFFS

Vera T.
Baldwin, Kansas

Here's yet another way to create a delight for the belly with mashed potatoes. If I didn't know better, I'd think my mom invented mashed potatoes, considerin' all the things she does with them. But everyone knows that Mrs. Mashed was the first to invent them.

What you need: 4 cups *hot* mashed potatoes
2 eggs, separated (the yolks from the whites, not from each other)
4 tbsp. milk
2 tbsp. butter
salt to taste
1/4 tsp. paprika

What to do: Make your plain mashed potatoes by boiling, drying, and mashing the spuds. Next, add the seasonings, milk, and butter. Mix in the well-beaten egg yolks, and then fold in the eggs whites, which have been beaten stiff (you'd be stiff, too, if you had been beaten this much.) Turn into a buttered baking dish and bake at 400° until brown — about 15 minutes.

69 *POTATOES AU GRATIN*

Ever wonder how to pronounce "au?" "Ow?" "Aw?" "Uh?" "Oh?" "None of the above?" Well, it's pronounced like the long "o" (like "Oh"). But this isn't an English book, it's a cook book, so fix up these spuds, and pronounce it any way you like.

What you need: 4-6 potatoes
1 onion, sliced, and in rings
1 cup milk, or half-and-half
2 tbsp. butter, melted
1 cup shredded cheese
1/2 cup bread crumbs
salt and pepper to taste

What to do: Slice potatoes thin. In a greased casserole dish, place a layer of potatoes, onion rings, and salt and pepper to taste. Fill the dish thusly to within 1 inch of the top. Pour milk (or half-and-half) over spuds, and spread cheese on top evenly. Now mix together the bread crumbs and melted butter. Sprinkle this over the cheese and place dish in a hot 425° oven until potatoes are tender — about 20 or 30 minutes, depending on how deep your dish of potatoes is.

70 *POTATOES O'BRIEN*

Vera T.
Baldwin, Kansas

This one has been around a while, and for good reason: good eating. With a fine Irish name like O'Brien, you'll probably want to garnish the dish with shamrocks.

What you need: 4 large potatoes
4 small onions or so

small slab salt pork
1/2 cup diced pimiento
salt and pepper to taste

What to do: Peel potatoes and slice very thin. Peel the outer skins from the onions and slice enough to equal one-half of the quantity of sliced spuds. Cube the salt pork and fry until done. Now add your onions and potatoes and enough water to cover the bottom of the pan. Cover tightly and simmer slowly, stirring occasionally. When tender, add pimiento, salt and pepper, and brown. Serve like an omelet.

POTATOES AND CHILIES   71

This South-of-the-border concoction sure hits the spot when you have to satisfy your *caliente* craving in the realm of spuddery.

What you need: 4 large potatoes, sliced
1-2 long green chilies (depending on your taste), chopped fine
1/2 onion, chopped
peanut oil
salt and pepper to taste
1/2 tsp. garlic powder

What to do: Cover the bottom of a skillet with peanut oil and add the potatoes, chilies, onion, and spices. Pour in about 1/4 cup water, cover, and cook over medium heat, stirring after 6 or 7 minutes. Be sure to leave the lid on at least this long before stirring so the potatoes and chilies will have a chance to steam and get acquainted. Once tender, remove the lid, increase the heat some and brown. Great with scrambled eggs and hot sauce.

72 *MUSHROOM CHOWDER*

You can tell I like chowder, huh? This one is equally as good as the others, providing, of course, that you like mushrooms. Give it a try.

What you need: 1 pound fresh mushrooms, sliced
1 cup diced potatoes
1 cup finely chopped celery
1/2 cup diced carrots
1/2 cup chopped onion (I use more because I'm an onion freak)
1/2 cup melted butter
1 tsp. salt
1/4-1/2 tsp. pepper
1 tsp. unbleached white flour
2 tbsp. water
3 cups chicken stock
1 cup milk
grated Parmesan cheese

What to do: Sauté the onions until tender in the butter, using that same big kettle. Add the vegetables, salt, pepper, and mushrooms. Cover and simmer for 15 to 20 minutes, or until veggies are tender. Combine the flour and water, mixing until smooth. Stir this into the kettle, add the chicken stock and simmer another 10 minutes. Now pour in the milk along with 1/4 cup of the Parmesan cheese. Yum is this getting good. Cook over low heat (but do not boil), until thoroughly heated. Sprinkle each serving with additional cheese when you dish it out.

73

SKILLET SALAD

Boy here's a meal in one that's a winner. Great for any meal with some whole wheat toast and a schooner of fresh O.J. This is not just for breakfast anymore.

What you need: 2 large potatoes, sliced fairly thin
1/2 onion, chopped
3 eggs, beaten
1 large tomato, diced
1/2-1 avocado, diced
1/2 tsp. garlic powder
salt and pepper to taste
peanut oil

What to do: Cover the bottom of a skillet with peanut oil. Add the sliced potatoes, onion, garlic, salt, pepper, and about 2 or 3 tbsp. water. Cover and cook over medium heat for 7 to 8 minutes. Stir and cook until tender. Now add your eggs and scramble together with the potatoes. When nearly done, dump in your tomato and avocado. You don't want to cook these, only warm them. Stir all together and serve hot. Garnish with your fork and dig in.

74

SAVORY POTATOES

Sometimes the simpler recipes are your favorites. This one could well be one of those for you, too. Don't neglect these easy ones for meals you ordinarily don't fix potatoes for. I mean, wouldn't it be nice to wake up for your midnight snack to the smell of these cooking in the kitchen?

What you need: 3 medium potatoes
                        1 onion, chopped fine
                        2 slices bacon, chopped fine
                        salt and pepper to taste

What to do: Slice the potatoes and cover with cold water for about 30 minutes. Drain and dry with whatever you dry potatoes with. In the meantime, you have been cooking slowly the onion and bacon. Add your cold potatoes and seasonings, cover skillet, and cook until potatoes are mealy — about 20 minutes.

VERA'S HASH   **75**

This one is a lot older than I am, and is not unique to my mom, I am sure. It is, however, an old favorite around our house, and a fond (continuing!) childhood memory.

What you need: 3 potatoes, cubed
                        1 pound lean ground beef
                        1 small onion, chopped
                        1 tsp. garlic powder
                        salt and pepper to taste
                        peanut oil

What to do: Cover the bottom of your skillet with peanut oil. Dump everything else in together, cover, and cook over a low to medium heat until potatoes are tender, stirring occasionally as needed. Remove lid, increase heat some, and brown.

76 *STILL ANOTHER CHOWDER*

Now you're beginning to think I've gone chowder crazy! Chowder is like country soup — you can put about anything in it you want. Ahhh, you may ask, "what is the difference between chowder and soup?" Don't ask.

What you need:
3 cups water
3 chicken bouillon cubes
1-1/2–2 cups de-boned fresh fish
4 medium potatoes, peeled and diced
1 medium onion, sliced
1 cup thinly sliced carrots
1/2 cup diced green pepper
1/3 cup butter
1/3 cup unbleached white flour
3-1/2 cups milk
4 cups (1 pound) shredded sharp Cheddar cheese
1 (2 oz.) jar pimiento, drained and sliced
1/4 tsp. hot sauce

What to do: Combine the water and bouillon cube in your now well-chowdered kettle, and bring to a boil. Add the vegetables and fish, cover, and simmer until the veggies are tender — about 12 minutes. Melt the butter in a pan. Blend in the flour and cook 1 minute. Gradually add the milk and continue cooking over medium heat until thickened, stirring constantly. Add the cheese and continue stirring until melted. Now combine the cheese sauce you just made, the pimiento, and the hot sauce (if you want it hotter, add some cayenne pepper or curry powder) into the vegetable mixture. Cook over low heat until thoroughly heated, being careful not to boil. And don't worry, this is the last chowder recipe.

77

SCALLOPED POTATOES

Vera T.
Baldwin, Kansas

I remember these from way back. Mom is one of those cooks who just does it, and so I present this recipe in her own vernacular, the way she would "do it" when cooking it!

What you need: potatoes
milk
bacon
butter
salt and pepper to taste

What to do: Cover the bottom of your pan with a layer of raw potatoes, thinly sliced and peeled. Sprinkle lightly with salt and pepper, and dot with butter. Continue layering potatoes and seasonings, and on top of the last layer, place thin slices of bacon. Pour milk into the dish until the potatoes are almost covered. Bake in a 350° oven until potatoes are done and the bacon delicately crisped and browned — about 1 hour.

DEVILED POTATO PATTIES

Vera T.
Baldwin, Kansas

This is a good one for any meal, and particularly outstanding in a country breakfast served with eggs and toast. It tastes better if you actually get to eat that country breakfast in the country...!

What you need: 4 cups shredded, boiled potatoes
3/4 cup chopped ham
3 tbsp. chopped onion
2 tbsp. unbleached white flour
2 tbsp. chopped parsley
1 tbsp. prepared mustard
salt to taste
1/4 cup butter
1/2 cup evaporated milk or light cream
1/4 tsp. garlic powder

What to do: Lightly toss together the potatoes, ham, onion, flour, parsley, mustard, salt, and garlic powder. Form into 6 patties. Brown one side slowly over low heat in the butter. Spoon evaporated milk or cream over the patties, cooking until it is absorbed and the bottom of the patties are crusty and brown. Turn and cook until the other side is crusty.

79 *SCALLOPED POTATOES WITH HAM*

Laurie McMahan
Encinitas, California

I procured this recipe from Laurie while practicing for a play her husband Ray wrote: *The Marshmallow Boy.* Realizing, then, I was truly part of a food family, I decided to remain a mild-mannered writer by day, and become — *Spudzap!!* — Spud Man, by night. Donning a flakey brown cape and dusty pixie boots, I pledge power to the potato promise: Potatoes, not rice, makes every meal nice.

What you need: 6 potatoes, peeled and thinly sliced
1/2 onion, peeled and thinly sliced, or chopped
1 cup ham, diced
1 cup shredded cheddar cheese
1 recipe white sauce:
    2 tbsp. butter, melted
    2 tbsp. flour, added and stirred
    1 cup milk, added and stirred until thickened
    salt and pepper to taste

What to do: Spread 1/2 of potatoes in bottom of greased baking dish, top with 1/2 of onions and 1/2 of ham. Pour 1/2 of white sauce over this. Repeat layers. Season with more salt and pepper, if desired. Cover and bake at 350° for 1 hour. Uncover and bake for another 1/2 hour. During this last 1/2 hour, sprinkle on the cheese.

80 *ZEPHYR POTATOES*

Who else — Vera T.
Baldwin, Kansas

Here's yet another mashed potato plot, with a name no one quite knows what it means. Don't worry about the name, however, since you won't be eating it.

What you need: 1 cup mashed potatoes
1/2 cup grated American cheese
1 cup milk
salt to taste
1/2 cup unbleached white flour
1/2 tsp. baking powder
peanut oil

What to do: Stir the potatoes, cheese, milk, and salt together. Combine the flour and baking powder, and add to the potato mixture. Flour the board well, dump out the potatoes onto it, and form into a square lump, keeping it as square as possible while rolling it out to a 1/4 inch thickness, sprinkling the top with flour as needed to prevent sticking. Cut with a knife into 1/2 inch squares. With a spatula, lift each square into a frying pan and sauté in enough oil to keep from sticking. When well browned on both sides, serve immediately.

GERMAN POTATO CUSTARD

Part of my family (Weingardner) dates back to old Munich (a long way to go for dates), and this German use of potatoes for dessert is great!

What you need: 3 cups warm mashed potatoes
4 tbsp. softened butter
3/4 cup honey
1 cup milk
4 egg yolks, beaten
1/4 tsp. salt
few drops vanilla
juice of 1 lemon
grated peel of 1 lemon
4 egg whites, beaten stiff

What to do: Grab a medium-sized bowl and mix together the mashed potatoes, butter, honey, vanilla, and salt. Blend until creamy. Combine the egg yolks, milk, lemon peel and juice, stirring together well, then adding to the potato mixture. Mix well, folding in the egg whites last. Pour into small dishes or a big one, making sure to grease well. Bake at 350° in a preheated oven for about 25 minutes. When nearly done, sprinkle top with nutmeg.

BAKED POTATO TOPPINGS

Having a baked potato party is great fun. Not only can everyone come dressed as their favorite baked potato, but you have the toasty tubers as the main course for dinner. If you were having the party, then you furnish all the baked potatoes, and everyone else would provide their favorite topping, other than the usual favorites of butter, sour cream, chives, bacon, and cheese (which you or some of your supporting cast can supply). A big pot of gumbo and salad cinches success for the evening. Give the Silver Spud Award for the most creative topping for the evening. The next few recipes are but starters for your stockpile of treasured toppings.

When it comes to baking potatoes, I am an anti-foiler. Generally speaking, I never wrap my spuds in foil for baking. I scrub them with a brisk brush under running water, poke holes in the skin with a fork, and plop into a hot oven. Be sure to poke holes in the skin to allow the steam to escape. This allows for a fluffy and mealy center, and avoids turning your baked potato into a potato grenade, which plasters the entire inside of your freshly-cleaned oven with exploding potato (you too, if you open the door at the wrong time). I like the no-foil method because I prefer to eat the potato skins, and like them slightly crisp, rather than moist and soggy. That is why I cook my baked potatoes at a higher temperature for a shorter period of time: 425° to 450°, until fork tender. Regardless of how I like them, you cook them the way that suits your's and your family's taste; that's the beauty of cooking: it's creative and fun, especially when done with someone you love, like a potato.

82 *HOT BROCCOLI TOPPING*

What you need: 2 cups cooked, fresh or frozen broccoli, chopped
1 large stalk celery, chopped
1/2 large onion, chopped
1 can cream of mushroom soup (although I prefer the fresh
    mushrooms, the cream and butter, and making my own)
1 cup grated cheddar cheese
1 tsp. garlic powder
Worcestershire sauce to taste
1 tbsp. butter
paprika

What to do: Drain and set aside your cooked broccoli. Sauté celery and onion in butter and Worcestershire sauce. Add the mushroom soup (canned or homemade), but do not dilute with water. Add the grated cheese and garlic (taste before adding garlic, since the canned soup may already be flavored with enough garlic), stirring frequently. Once cheese is melted, combine with the broccoli and mix together well. Heat until bubbly, increasing heat a little if necessary. When good and hot, scoop into hot serving dish, top with paprika, and get the spuds ready.

83 *SPICY AVOCADO TOPPING*

What you need: 2-3 avocados
1 tbsp. chopped onion (grated is best)
1 clove garlic, finely chopped or crushed
    (or 1 tbsp. garlic powder)

1 egg
1/2 tsp. dry mustard
1/2 cup peanut oil
1 "shake" Worcestershire sauce
1 tsp. lemon juice
1/4 tsp. Tabasco sauce
1/4 cup sour cream
salt and pepper to taste

What to do: In a blender, mix the egg and mustard, then adding the oil slowly while blending. Add seasonings and avocado, blending until smooth. Last, add your sour cream, mixing well. Cover and chill an hour or so, allowing flavors to blend. Before serving, stir.

CRAB TOPPING

84

What you need: 2 cups flaked crab meat (canned or fresh)
1-1/2 cups sour cream
1 tsp. chopped pimiento
1 tsp. garlic powder
2 tbsp. bacon grease
1 tbsp. chopped onion
salt and pepper to taste

What to do: Sauté onion and garlic in bacon grease. Remove and mix with sour cream, salt, pepper, and pimiento. Combine thoroughly, adding crab meat last to the well-blended ingredients. Mix well and serve chilled.

85 *WORLDS OF ONION TOPPING*

What you need: 2 onions
2-3 tbsp. Worcestershire sauce
1 clove garlic, crushed or minced
peanut oil
salt to taste

What to do: Be sure you like onions, first. If so, slice the onions and separate the rings. Cover the bottom of your skillet with peanut oil and add the garlic, salt, and Worcestershire sauce. Allow to cook briefly, then adding the onion rings, using more oil if needed. Cook onions over medium heat until they start to brown. Spoon over spuds and serve.

86 *CHICKEN 'N' MUSHROOMS TOPPING*

What you need: 1 cup boiled chicken, chopped fine
1/2 cup fresh mushrooms, chopped
1 cup sour cream
1/2 cup grated favorite cheese
1/2 onion, chopped fine
1 clove garlic, crushed or minced
salt and pepper to taste
1 tsp. Worcestershire sauce
1/4 to 1/2 tsp. paprika
peanut oil

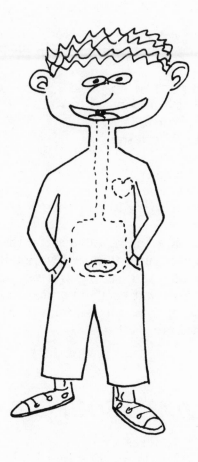

What to do: Sauté onion in peanut oil, garlic, and Worcestershire sauce, until starting to brown. Add sour cream and cheese, stirring over low heat to melt cheese. Do not boil. Add remaining ingredients and heat thoroughly. Spud time.

87
MORE SCALLOPED POTATOES

Here's another variation on a favorite theme. Not to be confused with "scalped potatoes" or the condition of a spud after it has been peeled.

What you need: 4-6 medium potatoes
1-1/2 onion, raw and sliced in rings
paprika for garnish
salt and pepper to taste
1-1/2 to 2 cups milk
1/2 cup sour cream
butter
1/4 cup finely-chopped bell pepper

What to do: Grease the bottom of a baking dish, scrub the spuds, and slice thinly. Put layers of potatoes and onion rings with a few scattered bell pepper pieces alternately in the dish until dish is full, salting and peppering each layer to taste. Combine the milk and sour cream and heat some (do not boil). When well mixed, pour over potatoes, onions, and pepper, garnish with paprika, and bake at 425° for about an hour, or until potatoes are tender.

88
POTATO SOUFFLÉ

Mrs. Frank K. Dunn
Charleston, Illinois

Here's a light and fluffy way to sling your spuds.

What you need: 2 heaping tbsp. mashed potatoes
3 eggs, separated

1 cup milk
pinch salt
1 tbsp. butter

What to do: Beat those little egg yolks real good. Now that your beatin' hand is warmed up, in a separate bowl, beat the egg whites until they're stiff (not too much or you'll be stiff). Now mix the egg yolks, potatoes, milk, salt, and butter together. Very carefully, fold in the stiffly-beaten egg whites. Bake in a buttered pan for 20 minutes or so, at 400°.

POTATO-PEANUT BUTTER CANDY **89**

Cheryl Wooten
Napa, California

Yes, you read right. This uses a lot of sugar, too, but is a great candy recipe. Serve this at your next party if you want to have the oddest but best candy in town. You will likewise be their oddest but best friend in town. . . .

What you need: 1 medium potato
1 pound (plus) sugar
peanut butter

What to do: Boil spud, peel it, and mash well. Add sugar to potato. This liquifies the potato for a short while, so work fast. On a sheet of waxed paper, spread some powdered sugar. Pour mixture on this and spread out. Now put on a thin layer of peanut butter and roll the whole thing up (not the waxed paper) like a jelly roll and cut into thin slices. Let harden, and there you have it!

90 *POTATO LOGS*

Ed Omens
La Jolla, California

Ed is from lumber-jack country, and everything they do there has to be associated with logs. It is only natural that Ed's favorite food would be potato logs. So chop your fork into some of these.

What you need: 4 or 5 potatoes
1 egg
1 tbsp. butter
salt and pepper to taste
1 cup crushed corn flakes

What to do: Boil the potatoes until done, mash, and mix with the egg, butter, salt and pepper to make mashed potatoes. Taking a 1/4 cup portion of the mashed spuds, shape into a "log" about 4 to 5 inches long and 1 inch or so in diameter. Roll each log in the corn flakes to coat. Bake on a lightly greased cookie sheet that you can now call a log sheet at 425° for 12 to 15 minutes, or until light brown.

91 *POTATO CEREAL*

This is a cereal that most grandmothers seem to know. It's surprisingly good, however, and on a cold morning or any morning when you want hot cereal, this stuff is great. If you are like many people and have to avoid wheat flour, this cereal fits the bill. Try it.

What you need: 2 large raw potatoes
2 tbsp. wheat bran
1 tbsp. wheat germ (be sure it's fresh)
4 cups water
1 tbsp. butter
1/2 cup cream

What to do: Heat the water to a boiling point, adding a small amount of salt if you desire. Shread the potatoes and dump into the boiling water. Add the bran. Stir together well, letting cook a minute or two. The potatoes will cook quickly depending on how fine you shredded them. Remove from the heat and let stand a few minutes. Scoop into a bowl, add butter, and pour on cream. Sprinkle wheat germ on top, and gobble away.

ZIPPY SCALLOPED POTATOES 92

Hazelle Carter

Everyone knows what scalloped potatoes are, so we thought you should have some with extra "zip" in them. I mean, a recipe can't come out of Texas without having a little something extra in it, can it?

What you need: 7-10 potatoes, boiled, diced
1/2 pound cheese, diced
1 green pepper, diced
1 medium onion, chopped
1/2 pound butter, melted
1 slice bread, diced
salt and pepper to taste
1 small jar pimiento
1 cup milk
1/4—1/2 tsp. cayenne pepper
1 clove garlic, crushed or minced
cornflakes

What to do: Mix ingredients except the cornflakes (being sure to use the pimiento *inside* the jar, and not the jar itself), and put into a buttered casserole dish. Sprinkle cornflakes on top and slide into your preheated 350° oven for 45 minutes.

93

FRENCH POTATO SOUP

Evelyn La Mar and Mary Molter
Sun City, California

Here's a super soup to sup. This recipe comes from two sisters I met one day at the La Valencia Hotel in La Jolla, California. I was holding the First Annual Spud Society Convention (by myself), and these two dear people happened by and became the first members. This is one of their recipes.

What you need: 4 green onions, sliced
2 cups thinly sliced potatoes
2 cups chicken broth
4 tbsp. butter
2 cups milk
chopped parsley

What to do: Sauté the green onions in butter for 3 minutes, then adding potatoes and chicken broth. Simmer until potatoes are tender — about 15 minutes. Sieve mixture through a food mill, or mash well with a masher. Now add milk and garnish with parsley. May be served hot or cold.

94

POTATO SOUP

Many a cold night has been made a bit warmer with a mug of this and some sour dough bread garlic toast. Having your feet propped up in front of the fire sure helps, too!

What you need: 4 large potatoes, raw
                      2 cups milk or cream
                      3 tbsp. butter
                      salt and pepper to taste
                      1 cup chicken stock
                      1 clove garlic
                      chopped chives

What to do: Dice potatoes and dump into a pan. Add chicken stock, the whole garlic clove, and enough water to cover the potatoes by an inch. Cover loosely, and cook until tender, checking to see that the spuds do not boil dry. I always make my soup thick, so pour in some more water if you need some. When the potatoes are done, discard the clove, and add the remaining ingredients except the chives. Simmer for 30 minutes and serve with the chives floating on top (be sure and get chives that can swim).

95

MOCK GUMBO

True gumbo generally does not contain potatoes and does contain okra. However, in the good old New Orleans tradition, I've concocted my own version using the best of both worlds, including that same Creole secret that goes into all Louisiana gumbos: the roux. This one is best after one or two reheatings.

What you need: 1 chicken, ready to cook
2 onions, chopped
8 potatoes
1/2—1 tsp. salt
3 carrots, sliced thin
3 stalks celery, sliced
2-3 cloves garlic, crushed
1 cup dry white wine
1 bay leaf
1/2-3/4 tsp. black pepper
1/2-3/4 tsp. cayenne pepper
1 tbsp. gumbo filé powder
1/4 tsp. ground cloves
1/4 tsp. nutmeg
1/4 tsp. thyme
2 tbsp. peanut oil
2 tbsp. unbleached white flour

What to do: Cut up the chicken and dump into a large kettle. Fill kettle half way to two-thirds full of water. Boil over medium-high heat until done. While the chicken is cooking, however, get out a skillet to make the roux. Into the skillet put 2 tbsp. peanut oil and 2 tbsp. flour. Always keep these proportions equal when making any quantity of roux. Brown this until it nearly burns, stirring constantly. You can smell it when the time is right (with practice!). Quickly add some of the chopped onion, stirring it through, followed by 1 cup *hot* stock from the kettle (make sure it is hot so the flour and oil mix immediately with the water). Cook down a bit. Pour into the kettle. Add everything else. When chicken is done, remove from the liquid, de-bone, chop into bite-size chunks, and return to the broth. Continue simmering until the potatoes are done. When ready to serve, remove bay leaf and discard. Dish out and rustle up some sour dough French bread, lots of butter, and a nice big salad. I hope you're ready to chow down!

96

POTATO BOATS

Mary E. Molter & Evelyn La Mar
Sun City, California

Everyone should have one of these at least once, if not to eat — then to float the rapids of the Snake River in Idaho. In regards to the eating side of their popularity, this recipe is timeless as the potato itself, and is a beautiful way to serve the spud.

What you need: As many large potatoes as there are people coming to dinner
(or breakfast or lunch)
scalded milk
butter
salt and pepper to taste
onion, chopped, or onion juice
grated favorite cheese

What to do: Scrub the spuds and bake until done. When tender, cut the top fourth off, being careful not to break the skins. With that same surgical skill, remove the white centers of all potatoes by scooping out carefully and dumping into a mixing bowl. Mash well, add your scalded milk (2 or 3 tbsp. per spud), 1 or 2 tbsp. butter per spud, salt and pepper to taste, your chopped onion, and maybe some of the cheese. Bits of bacon are sure good whipped in there. Now spoon this mixture back into the shells, piling up high. Cover the top with some more grated cheese, and place into a hot 375° oven for about 10 minutes, or until the potatoes are reheated and the cheese slightly browned on top.

97 CODFISH CAKES

Potatoes pescado . . . what a combination! If you happen to live in an area where codfish don't hang out, try any other favorite fish except hamburger. Be adventuresome.

What you need: 3 cups diced, raw potatoes
                       1-1/2 cups shredded codfish (fresh salmon is good)
                       1 egg, beaten
                       2 tbsp. butter, melted
                       1/4 tsp. black pepper
                       1/2 tsp. lemon juice
                       1 tbsp. grated onion
                       salt to taste
                       unbleached white flour
                             (with corn meal added, if preferred)

What to do: Plop the spuds into a kettle of boiling water until potatoes are tender. Meanwhile, simmer fish in another pan of water until tender — about 10 to 15 minutes. Drain and mash together with potatoes. Add the remaining ingredients except the flour, mixing thoroughly. Form into small patties. Coat with the flour (and cornmeal mixture if desired), and fry in hot oil until crispy. Drain and serve.

98 FRENCH FRIED POTATOES

Sherri T.

You've probably eaten thousands of these, but made nary a one. So here's how. Be you the All-American type and douse your fries in ketchup, British with your malt vinegar, or whomever — you'll love dipping and sopping all sorts of juices and dips with this old favorite.

What you need: potatoes
ice-cold water
oil or grease for cooking the potatoes
1/2 cup finely chopped chives
1/2 cup grated Gruyère cheese
salt to taste
1/2 cup red wine

What to do: Wash and maybe peel the potatoes. I like them left unpeeled. Cut into lengthwise slices of 1/4 to 1/2 inch thick, then again into 1/4 inch strips. Soak 30 minutes in ice-cold water, then dry. Heat oil or grease (enough to completely cover the potatoes) to 375°. Drop the spud strips into the hot grease and cook until tender and brown. Drain on absorbent paper and serve immediately with a side dip of the remaining ingredients. Most people prefer to salt the freshly cooked french fries as they come fresh out of the cooker. Be sure to re-heat the oil to 375° before adding another load of potatoes. The cold spuds lower the temperature of the grease and oil so they cook thoroughly without browning too soon.

99 *POTATO CORNBREAD*

Why have ordinary cornbread when you can have this?! Potato cornbread is good for breakfast with eggs and the works. It makes a great snack since it is so heavy (sticks to your ribs). I make it thin, which means it bakes hard and crispy. If you want a softer center, double the recipe.

What you need:
    1 cup grated potatoes
    2 tbsp. butter
    2 cups yellow cornmeal
    1/2 tsp. salt or less
    scant 1 tsp. baking powder
    1 egg, slightly beaten
    3/4 cup milk

What to do: Preheat oven to 375°. Squeeze out some of the liquid from the 1 cup of grated potatoes. Put the butter in a 12 inch cast iron skillet and set it in the oven, being careful to only melt the butter, not brown it. In a large bowl, mix together the cornmeal, salt, and baking powder. In another bowl, combine the egg and milk. Make a "well" in the center of the cornmeal and pour in the eggmilk. Stir until well blended. Now mix in the potatoes. Remove the skillet from the oven and gently tilt it so the butter coats the bottom and sides. Pour the cornbread batter in and spread it to completely cover the bottom of the skillet. Place in the oven and bake for 25 to 35 minutes or until done. Test thicker cornbreads by sticking a knife into the center. When it comes out clean and with no uncooked batter on it, it is done.

FISH PATTIES

Frying fish is not the only way to enjoy them. Swimming with them is another. To satisfy your hunger, try steaming them, poaching, baking, and broiling them. Never cook fish at boiling temperatures. Cooking fish at this high a temperature breaks down too much of the tissue, letting the nutritious juices and vitamins either run out or be destroyed, and leaving you with a rather tasteless and dry end product. To cook fish, do so quickly, rather than slowly as you do with meat. Here, we again team up fish with potatoes and other delights, to concoct another melange of cookery called a "pattie." (Chowders, soups, and hashes are others.) The ultimate point is to have fun making them, be creative, and enjoy the fruit of your labors!

What you need: 2 pounds cleaned fish (catfish, carp, etc.)
2-3 medium potatoes
3 eggs
1 medium onion, chopped in chunks
2 tsp. oregano
1 tsp. thyme
1 tsp. sage
1/2 tsp. garlic powder
salt and pepper to taste
4 tbsp. vinegar
4 tbsp. butter
1 tbsp. milk

What to do: Simmer the fish in a small amount of water for about 15 minutes, or until tender. At the same time, cut the potatoes into chunks and boil until done. Drain and keep warm. Take the fish (no bones) and toss into your blender with the eggs, and onion. Puree the contents. Be sure to do this to grind up any small bones escaping your eagle eye. Mash the potatoes and combine with the remaining ingredients except butter and milk. Add to pureed fish mixture and mix well. Put butter and milk into a large skillet over a medium heat. Make small patties out of the fish concoction and place into skillet. Cook until brown on bottom, turn, and brown the other side.

101 *POTATO PEELINGS*

Aha! You thought you were going to get away with throwing out the peelings from all those potatoes, didn't you? Having gone through the book non-stop, you should have a hefty mountain of skins all saved up in the backyard. I am not insensitive, however, so — yes — go ahead and let the compost pile have *a few* of them. With the rest, get ready for a great side dish that is a lot better tasting than potato chips from the store.

What you need: your mountain of saved potato peelings
salt to taste
garlic powder to taste
oil

What to do: Pat the peelings mostly dry with a paper towel. In a skillet (unless you have a deep-fat fryer), put 1/2 inch or so of oil. I like peanut oil because of the subtle flavor it adds to the peelings. Heat it hot enough so that a drop of water crackles when flicked in. Put only enough peelings into the grease so all can be covered with oil. Cook until crisp and brown — which isn't too long, so watch them. Remove, drain, and season to taste. Parmesan cheese sprinkled on top is also good, along with lots of other things only you could think up. Serve hot and enjoy.